what do
Wheels
and Cranks
do?

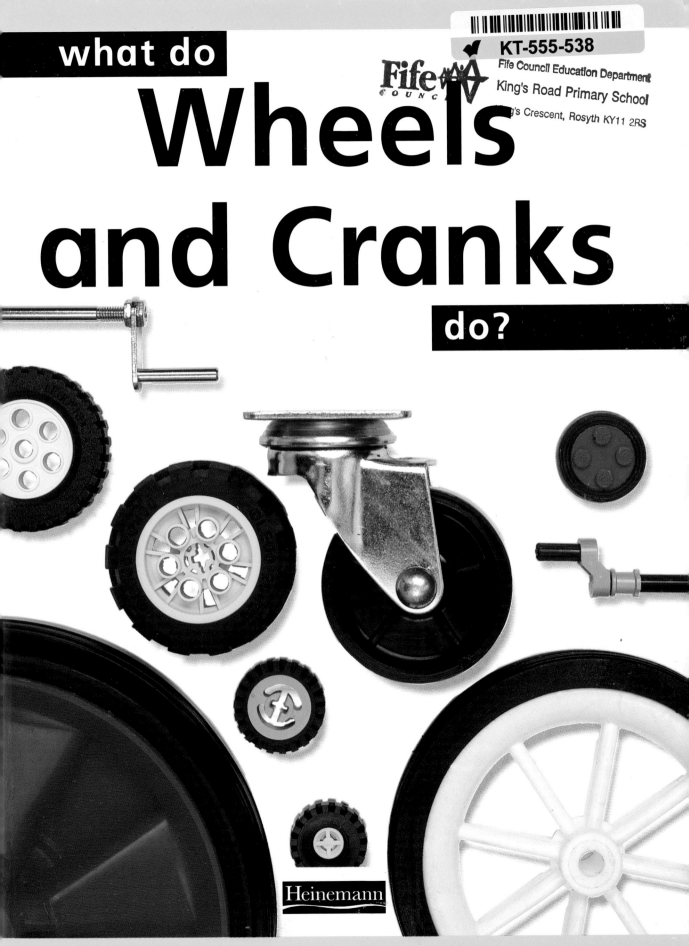

Heinemann

David Glover

First published in Great Britain by Heinemann Library
Halley Court, Jordan Hill, Oxford OX2 8EJ
a division of Reed Educational & Professional Publishing Ltd.

MELBOURNE AUCKLAND
FLORENCE PRAGUE MADRID ATHENS
SINGAPORE TOKYO SÃO PAULO
CHICAGO PORTSMOUTH NH MEXICO
IBADAN GABORONE JOHANNESBURG
KAMPALA NAIROBI

Designed by Celia Floyd and Sharon Rudd
Illustrated by Barry Atkinson (pp5, 17, 21), Douglas Hall (p6) and Tony Kenyon (p4)
Printed in Hong Kong / China

01
10 9 8 7 6 5

ISBN 0 431 06271 4
This title is also available in a hardback library edition (ISBN 0 431 06270 6).

British Library Cataloguing in Publication Data
Glover, David
   What do wheels and cranks do?
   1. Wheels – Juvenile literature 2. Cranks and crankshafts –
   Juvenile literature
   I. Title II. Wheels and cranks
   621.8 ' 27

Acknowledgements
The Publishers would like to thank the following for permission to reproduce photographs:
Trevor Clifford pp5, 6, 7, 19top, 22, 23; Zefa pp8, 9, 11, 15bottom, 18; Tony Stone Worldwide p10; Stockfile/Steven Behr p12; Lori Adamski Peek/TSW p13; TRIP/R Drury p14/ G Horner p20; Quadrant Picture Library p15top; Panos Pictures/ Ron Giling p16; Derek Cattani/Zefa p17; Mary Evans Picture Library p19; Collections/Brian Shuel p21.
Cover photograph by Trevor Clifford
Commissioned photography arranged by Hilary Fletcher
Special thanks to Rose who appears in the photographs.

Thanks to David Byrne for his comments on the initial draft.

The Publishers would like to thank Toys R Us Ltd The Worlds Biggest Toy Megastore, NES Arnold Ltd for the kind loan of equipment and material used in this book.

Contents

What are wheels and cranks?

Everyone knows what a wheel is. It is one of the most important **inventions** ever made. Wheels are round and they turn to make things go. There are wheels on toys, on bicycles, trains, cars and lorries.

If no one had invented the wheel we would have to walk everywhere. We would need to carry things on our backs or drag them along the ground.

crank handle

turn

If you put a handle on one side of a wheel then you can use it to turn the wheel. This handle is called a crank. Sometimes a crank handle is just a bent bar.

You turn a crank handle to work this pencil sharpener.

Rollers

This girl is learning how to walk on a barrel. The barrel rolls along under her feet.

You can move a heavy load on rollers. The ancient Egyptians built the pyramids by dragging huge stones on rollers. The rollers were made from tree trunks.

You can do the same thing using pencils to move a book. When one pencil is uncovered behind as the book moves forwards, pick it up and move it to the front.

FACT

From rollers to wheels

Long ago, the use of rollers probably gave people the idea for the first wheels.

FILE

Cart and car wheels

The wheels on this old cart are
made from wood. Wheels like this
have been made for hundreds of
years. A metal hoop is fixed
around the wheel to stop it
wearing away. These wheels give
a very bumpy ride.

A modern car wheel has a thick rubber **tyre** wrapped around it. The tyre is filled with air, like a balloon. This helps the tyre to bounce over bumps on the road.

The pattern that is cut into a tyre is called the **tread**. The tread helps the tyre to **grip** on wet roads.

Bicycle wheels

A racing bicycle has very light-weight wheels. Thin wire **spokes** hold the **rim** of the wheel in place. Wheels like these are good for riding fast on smooth road surfaces.

A mountain bike has much thicker wheels than a racing bike. They are heavier and make the bike slower, but they are stronger. Wheels like these are good for riding over rough ground.

A smooth ride

Big wheels give a smoother ride than small wheels. Imagine a bicycle with tiny roller-skate wheels. It would soon make you *saddle sore*!

Boards and blades

A skateboard has two pairs of small rubber wheels. Each wheel spins round on a rod. This rod is called an **axle**. Inside the wheels are small metal balls called **ball bearings**. They make the wheels turn smoothly.

These roller blades have four hard plastic wheels in a row. The **stiff** boots help you to balance. They stop you from twisting your ankles. An expert roller blader can go as fast as a person on a bicycle.

Skating tip

Skateboards and roller blades go best on smooth hard ground. Their small wheels don't work well on grass or mud.

Tractor and truck wheels

Tractor wheels have big tyres to stop them sinking in soft mud. The deep **tread** on the tyres gives extra **grip** when the ground is slippery.

This truck can go almost anywhere on its huge wheels. It can drive through deep water and climb steep hills. It can even drive over other trucks!

FACT

Giant trucks

The biggest tyres in the world are twice as tall as a man. They are fitted to giant dumper trucks.

FILE

Crank handles

This machine is used for crushing
sugar cane to squeeze out the
juice. The mules are turning the
crank handle as they walk round.
This makes the rollers turn and
crush the cane.

There is a crank handle on this old car. You turn the handle to get the engine going. Modern cars have a separate starter **motor** that is worked by turning a key.

crank handle

crank handle

crank handle

Records and movies

The first record players and the first movie cameras had crank handles to make them work. Modern machines use electric motors to make things turn.

Pedal power

This woman turns her spinning wheel by pedalling with her foot. The pedal pushes a crank to make the wheel turn round.

Cranks make pedal cars go. First you push one pedal, then the other. Your pushes turn the crank, and the crank turns the car's wheels.

Cranky cycles

The very first bicycles were worked by cranks. The cyclist pushed the pedal down to make the wheels turn.

Crank it up!

A canal **lock** is worked by a crank handle. The lock keeper turns the handle to let water in or out of the lock. The handle opens a hole in the lock gate to let the water through.

An organ grinder turns a crank handle to make music. His organ plays tunes as he winds the handle. The quicker he turns the handle, the faster the music plays.

Winding up

The handle on a water well is a crank. It winds up the rope to lift the bucket.

crank handle

Cranky toys

This garden toy works when the wind blows. The wind makes the windmill turn. The windmill turns a crank to make the man wind up the bucket from the well.

A crank turns the wheel on this model steam engine. The steam pushes a **rod** inside a tube. This rod is called a **piston**. The piston pushes the crank and the wheel turns round.

crank   piston

Glossary

axle   The rod or bar in the middle of a wheel.

ball bearings   Small metal balls inside a wheel which make it turn smoothly.

grip   To hold tightly.

inventions   Ideas for new machines that no one has made before.

lock   An invention that stops you opening a door or a lid unless you have a special key.

motor   A machine that uses electricity or fuels such as petrol or coal to make things move.

piston   A rod inside a tube, which is pushed by steam to make a crank turn.

rim   The outside part or edge of a wheel.

rod   A bar or stick, often made from metal.

saddle sore   Feeling uncomfortable after sitting on a hard seat or saddle for too long!

spokes   Metal wires that hold the rim of a bicycle wheel in place.

stiff   Difficult to bend.

tread   The pattern in a rubber tyre that helps it grip the road when it is wet or muddy.

tyre   The rubber ring put around the rim of a wheel.

Index